First published in 2005 by Grolier
An imprint of Scholastic Library Publishing
Old Sherman Turnpike
Danbury, Connecticut 06816

For information address the publisher:
Scholastic Library Publishing, Old Sherman Turnpike,
Danbury, Connecticut 06816

Library of Congress Cataloging-in-Publication Data

Arnold, James R.
    The industrial revolution / James R. Arnold and Roberta Wiener.
      p. cm
    Includes bibliographical references and index.
    Contents: v. 1. A turning point in history – v. 2. The industrial
revolution begins – v. 3. The industrial revolution spreads – v. 4. The
industrial revolution comes to America – v. 5. The growth of the
industrial revolution in America – v. 6. The industrial revolution
spreads through Europe – v. 7. The worldwide industrial revolution –
v. 8. America's second industrial revolution – v. 9. The industrial
revolution and the working class v. 10. The industrial revolution and
American society.
      ISBN 0-7172-6031-3 (set)—ISBN 0-7172-6032-1 (v. 1)—
    ISBN 0-7172-6033-X (v. 2)—ISBN 0-7172-6034-8 (v. 3)—
    ISBN 0-7172-6035-6 (v. 4)—ISBN 0-7172-6036-4 (v. 5)—
    ISBN 0-7172-6037-2 (v. 6)—ISBN 0-7172-6038-0 (v. 7)—
    ISBN 0-7172-6039-9 (v. 8)—ISBN 0-7172-6040-2 (v. 9)—
    ISBN 0-7172-6041-0 (v. 10)
      1. Industrial revolution. 2. Economic history. I. Wiener, Roberta.
II. Title.

HD2321.A73 2005
330.9'034–dc22   2004054243

Printed and bound in China

CONTENTS

West and East

The Industrial Revolution began in England during the eighteenth century and then spread to other parts of the world. Britain's industrial development resulted from the growth and rapid spread of interrelated innovations in manufacturing technology. The distinctive growing points of the process were in the cotton, iron, engineering, machine tool, and transport industries. The pace of innovation in those sectors was spectacular.

The Industrial Revolution first spread to western Europe and the United States, and then gradually expanded elsewhere. It can be viewed as a series of waves flowing outward from Great Britain and carrying invention and innovation to distant shores. After lapping over western Europe, industrialization spread first to central Europe and later to eastern and southern Europe. The progress that had been made in western Europe and Great Britain forced the traditional industrialists in each of those regions to innovate or go under.

A Backward Region

Compared to western Europe and particularly compared to Great Britain, eastern and southern Europe had inefficient,

Great Britain developed roads, canals, and railroads to link producers with markets. Railroads especially promoted industrialization both by allowing industrialists in western Europe access to cheaper east European raw materials and by opening up new markets for their products.

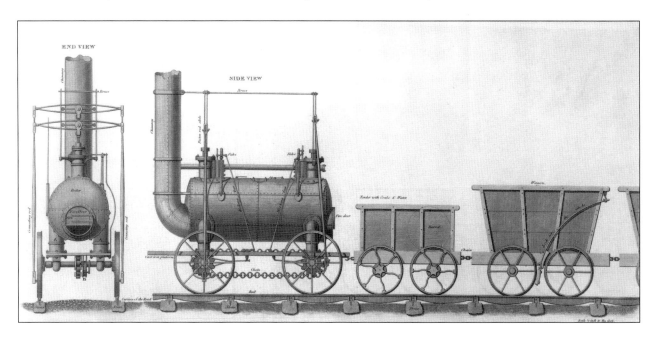

poverty-stricken agricultural sectors. Just as the rural poor of western Europe had been less well off than those in Great Britain, so the rural poor of eastern and southern Europe were worse off than those in western Europe.

A German army officer traveled down the Danube River in 1835. When he needed to move overland, he found the only available vehicle was "like a child's wagon...so short and narrow that one man could hardly sit in it." The entire vehicle including the hub and axle was made of wood. The region was so poor that even the horse's harness lacked metal of any sort. It was as if the officer had stepped into a time machine and emerged in ancient, preindustrial times.

The agricultural sector in places like the southern Danube River basin, Hungary, Russia, Italy, and Spain operated in much the same way as it had since the Middle Ages. Instead of providing an impetus for industrialization, as had been the case in Great Britain, the primitive agricultural sector delayed it.

The Danube River is the second longest river in Europe, running more than 1,700 miles from Germany through eastern Europe to the Black Sea.

THE "SECOND COMERS"

The first wave of industrialization had lapped over parts of western Europe before running out of momentum. Belgium, France, and Germany were "the first comers" to the Industrial Revolution. The "second comers" included the Netherlands, Switzerland, and Sweden.

THE NETHERLANDS

Each nation responded to the Industrial Revolution according to its own special circumstances.

European industrialization:
See also
Volume 3 pages 34–56

Merchants set up shipping offices in the Netherlands to conduct overseas trade.

The house of a high-ranking Dutch official in Java, in 1854. European colonial officials lived comfortably in their far-flung colonies

DEPRESSION: decrease in business activity, accompanied by unemployment and lower prices and earnings

For instance, although they were close neighbors, the Netherlands had an entirely different experience than Belgium during the opening decades of the Industrial Revolution.

In the 1600s the Netherlands had been the commercial and industrial center of the world. During the next century it gradually began to fall behind England, but it still had an efficient agriculture, a good transport net, skilled workforce, and sophisticated financial sector. Dutch society at least matched England in terms of urbanization and wealth, while it exceeded England in overall literacy. By 1810 about 28 percent of the male labor force worked in industry, a number very similar to Great Britain at that time.

The economic health of the Netherlands relied on overseas trade, particularly with its colonies. Its processing industries such as sugar refining, paper making, and gin distillation were concentrated around its ports. To prosper they depended on the import of raw materials and the export of finished goods. The Napoleonic Wars (1792-1815) caused the Netherlands to experience a deep **depression**. The French dominated the country between 1795 and 1814, and put an end to Dutch overseas trade. Meanwhile, England captured the country's overseas colonies. Deprived of raw materials and denied exports, much Dutch industry came to a halt.

The Netherlands was slow to recover from the wars. In addition, the country's social and political structure remained stuck in an age long passed, the glory years of the 1600s. When the Netherlands and Belgium separated in 1830, industrial growth finally took off.

The impetus for that growth was the exploitation of the

Dutch colony in Java. Javanese peasants got very low wages for cultivating export products, such as coffee and sugar, for the colonial government. The Dutch government used those cheap imports to stimulate the home economy while protecting its emerging industries with tariffs.

As a result, the first significant industrialization using steam engines took place in the Amsterdam sugar-refining industry. Mechanization slowly spread to such industries as ship building and textiles, all of it based on trade with Java. Until about 1855 colonial trade dominated industrial growth in the Netherlands.

Javanese workers tapping rubber trees, source of one of the important raw materials exported from Java.

Amsterdam was the Netherlands' center for trade and industry.

Aside from the sugar-refining industry, steam power spread slowly in the Netherlands. In the textile industry, which had led the way in England some 70 years before, large-scale industry did not replace cottage industries until the period from 1850 to 1880. Instead, small and medium industries continued to dominate the economy, with the traditional agricultural processing industries playing the leading role. Modern industrialization did not take firm hold in the Netherlands until after 1890.

SWITZERLAND

A distinct combination of natural and manmade obstacles blocked Switzerland's path to industrialization. Switzerland was a small, mountainous, landlocked region with few natural resources and limited iron and coal. Until 1848 the land was not even a nation but rather a loose collection of cantons (somewhat like large counties), with each canton having the right to mint money, regulate trade, define weights and measures, and set tariffs on trade. Consequently, there was no national market.

Watch- and clockmaking were specialized trades requiring knowledge and skill. Meticulous craftsmanship and a fine sense of style made Swiss watches the world leaders. By 1850 the area around Geneva was responsible for two-thirds of the entire world's production.

Clocks:
See also
Volume 4 pages 47, 49–50

Fifty years of political turmoil led to a federal constitution in 1848 under which the cantons retained their sovereignty but gave up economic rights so that a national market could come into being. The nineteenth-century French historian Alexis de Tocqueville described the birth of modern Switzerland: "One people, composed of several races, speaking several languages, with several religious beliefs, various dissident sects, two churches both equally established and privileged...two societies, one very old and the other very young, joined in marriage in spite of the age difference."

Before the Industrial Revolution began in England, Switzerland had some industry, including watch, and clock-making and textile manufacture. During the eighteenth century "cotton mania" swept the country, with cotton replacing traditional linen and silk manufacture as the most important sector in the textile industry. In 1785 Swiss merchants started to import machine-manufactured yarn from England. Until that time hand spinning was an important cottage industry throughout much of Switzerland. The yarn imports marked the beginning of a long and painful economic decline for hand spinners.

In 1800 the nation employed about 140,000 textile workers, and at least 100,000 of them worked with cotton. The next year the first Swiss spinning mill using machinery, based on Crompton's mule (see Volume 2), went into operation. As was the case elsewhere, neither the home spinner nor the traditional small spinning mills could compete with large factories. Tens of thousands of workers lost their jobs.

By 1830 came the mechanization of cotton weaving. Hand weavers feared that they too would lose their jobs. Switzerland experienced protests like the "Luddite" movement in England (see Volume 2), with weavers burning to the ground a weaving mill as soon as it was built. In contrast to what took place in England, worker protest considerably slowed the pace of industrialization. Between 1850 and 1867, a period when mechanical weaving was well established in more industrialized nations, Switzerland employed more hand weavers than at any other time in its history.

To compete effectively in the world market, Switzerland worked to avoid direct competition

Switzerland's textile industry was slow to adopt mechanical looms.

with foreign manufacturers, particularly competition with mass-produced English products, and instead concentrated on specialty items for the export trade. Toward that goal the watch- and clockmaking and textile industries exported more than 90 percent of their manufactures during the first half of the nineteenth century.

By 1850 Switzerland occupied its own economic niche. It had well-developed, highly efficient light industries that were not dominated by English competition. At the same time, it lacked a vigorous national market and instead had, at best, a very loose association of regional markets. The cantons finally addressed the lack of a national market by joining together to write the Constitution of 1848. Until that constitution the cantons failed to cooperate to do things, such as building a national railroad, that could stimulate industrialization.

Finally, around 1885 long-term, self-sustaining economic growth began, and Switzerland moved toward becoming a truly industrialized country. The industrial companies for which Switzerland today remains best known—the food-processing industries that gave the world Swiss chocolate and the chemical and drug industries that made companies like Hoffmann-La Roche and CIBA international pace setters—took off during the 1880s.

SWEDEN

On the eve of the Industrial Revolution in England, around the year 1760, Sweden was one of the poorest countries in Europe. Just as was the case in England, increased efficiency in the

When the American inventor Cyrus McCormick first exhibited his mechanical reaper in England in 1851, viewers made fun of its appearance. However, it won the grand prize of the exhibition and soon found customers throughout Europe and around the world.

A Leicester Improved Breed sheep. Farmers experimented with breeding different types of sheep to create breeds that produced more and better wool.

COMMON OR COMMONS: land in or around a village that any inhabitant may use

ENCLOSURE: placing a physical barrier, such as a fence, around a piece of farmland to mark it as private property

Some of the tasks of wool production, such as shearing sheep and washing the fleece, were not mechanized.

agricultural sector was a vital first step toward industrial development. Also as in England, that efficiency came from the **enclosure** of the **commons** (see Volume 1). As a result of the enclosure movement, the output of grain and potatoes increased 210 percent between 1800 and 1850 at a time when the rural population increased by only 50 percent.

The agricultural revolution prepared the way for an industrial revolution by providing a food surplus to support people working in nonagricultural occupations. It also created a market for iron farm tools as well as sowing, reaping, and threshing machines. Improved and increased sheep husbandry provided the raw wool for the Swedish textile industry to expand. Last, the increased prosperity enjoyed by farmers helped create a larger home market for a variety of manufactured items.

The earliest evidence of a blast furnace in Europe—dating back to about 1350—was found in Sweden.

Blast furnaces:
See also
Volume 2 page 35
Volume 4 pages 14–16

Charcoal:
See also
Volume 4 pages 62–63

CHARCOAL: a fuel made by charring wood in a buried fire so that very little air enters the fire

COKE: a form of coal that has been heated up to remove gases, so that it burns with great heat and little smoke

PUDDLING: a process for converting pig iron to wrought iron by melting and stirring it

SMELTING: melting metal ore to extract the pure metal

Sweden experienced its first phase of industrial expansion between 1830 and 1850, with the textile industry leading the way. The beginning of that period saw the introduction of cotton spinning mills and the expansion of the traditional woolen factories. Factory weaving did not arrive until about 1850. Until that time weaving remained a cottage industry.

The iron industry also partially modernized over that twenty-year span. The western world preferred to use Swedish pig iron for cutting tools because of its higher quality. That quality did not come from any special Swedish knowledge about iron **smelting** but rather from the purer ore mined in Sweden.

Swedish ironmasters struggled to adopt Cort's **puddling** processes (see Volume 2) and made limited progress in producing **coke** blast iron. Simultaneously, Swedish technicians improved some traditional techniques that relied on the country's abundant forests to make **charcoal** iron. Between 1825 and 1855 the production of cast iron and manufactured iron and steel doubled.

Beginning in 1850, steam power was introduced to the sawmill industry. In the past sawmills had used water power. That had limited where they could be located and caused them to close down during the long, frozen Swedish winter. Steam power propelled the sawmill industry to the forefront of Swedish industrialization. Sawmills could be built on the coast, which made it easier to export sawn products overseas, and they could operate year round. During the 1840s England opened up its markets, allowing the export of Swedish wood products to the entire British Empire. In 1840 the wood industries contributed about five percent of total national industrial output. By 1880 half of the nation's large sawmills used steam power, and the wood industries contributed 20 percent of total national industrial output, most of which was exported.

Sweden also made significant institutional reforms that stimulated industrialization. Between about 1850 and 1865 it abolished the guilds, which had strictly controlled crafts and trades, removed restrictions on imports and exports, reduced customs duties, and in general did away with trade regulations.

Obstacles to industrialization remained. Until the end of the nineteenth century Sweden lacked a capital market to provide business loans. Merchants financed industrialization with the profits from their businesses or by personal loans. As a result,

firms usually had to wait a long time to be paid for deliveries and were less willing to supply expensive items like factory machines. When the railway boom came to Sweden, foreign loans had to be secured to finance railroad construction.

Sweden took significant steps during its first phase of industrialization. Its textile industry became partially mechanized. The sawmill industry experienced explosive growth. Mining and metal industries made solid progress. Institutional reforms were put in place that would stimulate later economic development. But important steps were missing: Few industries were mechanized, and machinery was unevenly distributed within them; investment remained low; modern business organization and accounting had yet to take hold; and a modern banking industry was absent. Last, Sweden had not yet built the roads, harbors, and railways necessary for a modern industrial nation. A demonstration of Sweden's still poor and underdeveloped status came at the end of the 1860s, when northern Sweden suffered a harvest failure that led to widespread hunger.

That failure proved to be Sweden's last famine. The next 30 years from 1880 to 1910 witnessed a second phase of industrialization that transformed Sweden into a real industrial nation.

Sawmills:
See also
Volume 8 pages 8–9

Despite industrial development in Sweden, some areas were overpopulated, and people still lived in poverty. During the late 1800s more than three-quarters of a million Swedes emigrated to the United States, where many established farms on the prairies.

IN SEARCH OF A BETTER LIFE

During the 50-year period from 1860 to 1910 more than 22 million immigrants—most of them Europeans—entered the United States.

Europeans who lived on the lower rungs of the economic ladder encountered immovable obstacles to improving their lot in life. Foremost was the inability to own land. The wealthy owned large estates, while tenant farmers paid rent and scratched out a living on land they could never own.

Population growth among the rural poor in Europe, combined with the replacement of rural handicrafts by manufactured goods, led to high rates of unemployment. The unemployed migrated first to the cities to search for industrial jobs. Industrialization deprived handicraft workers of their livelihoods without creating enough jobs to employ them. The lack of jobs was particularly acute in southern and eastern Europe, where industrialization proceeded at a slower pace. Many unemployed or struggling workers then turned their attention to the growing economy on the far side of the Atlantic Ocean.

A series of disastrous potato blights in Ireland led to famine. As result, more than a million Irish people emigrated to America. Sweden and Germany both suffered from unemployment. For example, the number of people who left Sweden for America was higher than the number of industrial jobs available in all of Sweden. However, the wave of northern and western European immigration into America had peaked by 1890 and was followed by waves of immigration from southern and eastern Europe, the latecomers to the Industrial Revolution.

Immigrants worked long hours for low wages in the American textile and other industries. Even so, many had a higher standard of living than they had in Europe and entertained hopes of improving their lives even more. An eastern European man who entered the United States in 1914 went to work as a weaver. He eventually saved enough to open his own store. He recalled, "I never dreamed to stay in this place so long. I like it because, well, the place where I was born was worse than this....When I came here I didn't have nothing. At least now I have my own house.... And beside that, I put four children through university."

COUNTRY OF BIRTH: FOREIGN BORN POPULATION OF THE UNITED STATES (number of people in millions)		
	1860	1910
Total U.S. Population	31.0	91.0
Place of Birth		
Germany	0.6	2.3
Ireland	0.9	1.3
Sweden	*	0.6
Southern Europe (Greece, Italy, Spain, Portugal)	*	1.6
Eastern Europe (including Austria through Russia)	*	3.6
Europe - Total (in millions)	1.5	9.4
* = fewer than 100,000		

Opposite Top: An Italian family sewing garments at home. New England textile mills employed not only Irish but Swedish, Italian, Greek, Portuguese, Russian, and eastern European workers. Other immigrants labored in New York City sweat shops or did poorly paid piecework at home.

Opposite Bottom Left: Portuguese mill workers. One immigrant from southern Europe reported, "When I was in Portugal, no good. Too much work for no money. I like over here because of the money."

Opposite Bottom Right: Immigrants were not permitted to live in the same boarding houses as New England-born mill workers. In one mill town more than 300 people shared 48 small, windowless apartments.

THE INDUSTRIAL REVOLUTION IN SOUTHERN EUROPE

Northern European nations, and most especially England, experienced an agricultural revolution before the Industrial Revolution. The agricultural revolution began in the Middle Ages and expanded in the subsequent centuries. Most of the early European agricultural innovations that provided the basis for the revolution were only appropriate to northern European conditions. For example, the heavy plow revolutionized agriculture beginning in the sixth century by allowing farmers to clear the forests of fertile northwest Europe, but it was not useful for the lighter and sandier soils of southern Europe. In Italy, Spain, and Portugal farmers continued to use a light plow that was virtually unchanged

from Roman times. Likewise, while northern European farmers experimented with new crops, fertilizers, and methods of crop rotation, most of those innovations had not been introduced in much of southern Europe.

SPAIN

Spain had been a great power during the centuries preceding the Industrial Revolution. A large part of its wealth came from the exploitation of colonies in Central and South America. As was the case in the Netherlands, the Napoleonic Wars hit hard at Spain's economy. At various times Spain was at war either with England or with France. While Spain was at war with Great Britain, the Royal Navy targeted Spanish overseas colonies and foreign trade, on which the Spanish economy heavily depended. After Spain allied itself with Great Britain, French armies invaded and occupied much of Spain. During the period 1808 to 1814 the Spanish government teetered on the edge of collapse while the Spanish economy remained practically frozen in time. When the wars ended in 1815, the advances of the Industrial Revolution gave many British products an insurmountable competitive advantage to which Spain had no answer.

Only with great difficulty could farmers scratch a living out of the dry, rocky soil of central Spain.

Spain's geography also impeded its advance toward industrialization. Its sheer size made it different from countries like England or Belgium. The high, dry central plateau that split the country was not a prime agricultural region. Most people who lived within that large region survived at a mere subsistence level. The death rate was high, the birthrate low, so there was not a surplus population willing to move to urban areas and labor in factories. Also, transportation across the central plateau was difficult and expensive. As a result, that region remained isolated from trade and failed to create a prosperous home market for industrial products.

Compared to the other European nations that participated in the Industrial Revolution during the nineteenth century, the Spanish economy stagnated. Its people remained poor, and as late as 1900 about half could not read. Because of historical, geographical, and cultural factors modern industrialization did not take place in Spain until the twentieth century.

Italy was formed in 1870 by the unification of several independent states and republics.

ITALY IN 1860

N

| 0 | Miles | 50 |
| 0 | Kms | 80 |

TYROL
LOMBARDY
VENETIA
Istria
SARDINIA
Parma
Modena
TUSCANY
PAPAL STATES
Corsica
Sardinia
ADRIATIC SEA
TYRRHENIAN SEA
Kingdom of the TWO SICILIES
MEDITERRANEAN SEA

ITALY

Every nation had its own story about its path to industrialization. The Italian story was particularly surprising because, in times past, it seemed to be very well positioned to enter the new industrial world. In the fifteenth and sixteenth centuries Florence had been Europe's leading financial center. By the sixteenth century the surrounding plains had vast farms created on drained and diked lands with fields practicing continuous crop rotation. The Po River valley of Northern Italy had a fine canal network. Venice was the site of a shipbuilding center that received raw materials—hemp, wood, cloth—via those canals and employed thousands of workers to build ships that carried Italian goods all around the Mediterranean basin. The manufacture of glass, mirrors, dyes, luxury soaps, and silks made Venice the largest industrial city in Europe. In 1474 the Venetian Republic became the first place in Europe to encourage innovation by passing a bill providing for industrial patents.

The city-states of northern Italy made up the most highly urbanized and developed region of Europe. The mechanization of the Italian silk industry occurred before English inventors made the machines that propelled the takeoff of the textile industry and the ensuing Industrial Revolution. However,

Venetian glass took some unusual forms: One was spun glass, which was used to weave baskets.

English and French competitors began to challenge the Italian dominance of the silk industry during the eighteenth century. With the help of Italian bankers the French city of Lyons became the major weaving center in Europe. Furthermore, silk was a luxury good and subject to the whims of fashion, and in matters of style consumers looked to Paris. The popular expression arose "Parisian style made in Lyons."

When the Industrial Revolution began in England, the old Italian industrial centers were in decline, although they still retained a presence in international markets. But to an increasing extent they exported silk thread to the new weaving centers across the Alps, and thread exports were far less profitable than exporting woven silk. The reduction in profits meant that less money was available for Italian capitalists to invest in the new textile machinery being developed in England. Thus Italy presented an unusual case: With the silk industry it had a factory system before any other nation, but it was unable to use its advantage to build an industrialized economy.

Italian city streets bustled with economic activity.

THE SILK-THROWING FACTORY

The long, continuous filaments of silk presented a different technical problem than short wool, cotton, and linen fibers. The other fibers were gathered into a single strand by spinning. In contrast, silk filaments had to be processed by throwing: the twisting together of two or more long filaments to make a heavier and stronger thread.

Ever since the thirteenth century the Po River valley was the European center of the silk industry. In the hilly areas peasants tended the mulberry trees that the silk worms fed on. Women and children did the tedious hand labor of reeling, throwing, winding, and doubling the silk thread. In the fourteenth century Italian technicians in Bologna developed a mechanical method of reeling the silk thread off the silkworm cocoon. Although the silk-throwing machines were very complex, they were much more efficient, could be powered by moving water, and produced a higher-quality thread than that twisted by hand.

Just like the later English manufacturers in the cotton industry, the Bolognese silk manufacturers tried to keep the technology of their silk mills secret. However, industrial spies stole the secret, and soon silk mills sprung up throughout the Po River valley.

In the sixteenth century technicians added mechanical winders to the silk-throwing mills. Each mill stood two or three stories high and employed dozens of workers. The workers' jobs involved feeding the raw silk into the machines, knotting the threads when they broke (a chore usually done by children), controlling the twist points (a critical job done by adults), and loading the twisted thread into baskets. The early Italian silk mills worked on a factory system that predated Arkwright's cotton factories (see Volume 2) by at least 150 years.

By the end of the 1600s Bolognese technicians were building huge mills that employed about 300 workers. In another act of industrial espionage the Englishman John Lombe studied the Italian silk-throwing machines and returned home to build his own silk mill in Derby (see Volume 1 page 35).

Above: A moth laying eggs on a mulberry leaf. The life cycle of the silkworm begins with moths laying eggs. From the eggs hatch silkworms, which feed on mulberry leaves. The silkworms spin cocoons and stay inside the cocoons until they change into moths. Silk producers unwind the fibers that make up the cocoons and then twist the fibers into silk thread.

Left: Silk thread was wound onto large mechanical reels.

By 1800 the economy of northern Italy, where most industry was concentrated, was fast losing ground to the new English industries and to competitors in France, Belgium, and Germany. The Napoleonic Wars, many of whose campaigns took place on Italian soil, worsened the situation. After Napoleon's defeat in 1815 came a long period of Austrian occupation and domination of northern Italy. Another period of struggle, the Wars of Italian Unification, took place in the 1860s. The combination of Austrian dominance and subsequent war retarded Italy's progress toward a modern, industrial economy.

Italy had pockets of development. "English style" industrialization of the Italian textile industry took off after 1848. By 1861 cotton-spinning and silk-throwing factories employed some 200,000 workers. Turin, Milan, and Naples

emerged as major industrial centers specializing in the manufacture of textile machinery, printing presses, and agricultural machinery. But the iron and steel industries were badly obsolete, while the chemical industry consisted of small workshops limited to the production of gas for lighting.

By 1870 Italy stood on the ladder of economic development somewhere between the more industrialized countries of Great Britain, France, Belgium, and Germany and the less industrialized nations in the rest of Europe. In the future, competition from nearby Switzerland as well as France and Germany would force Italian entrepreneurs to modernize or perish. In the event, Italy's most impressive phase of industrial growth did not being until 1898. Even after that date a great divide remained between the more prosperous, industrialized northwest and the poor, agricultural south.

Italy's manufacturers could not begin to fulfill the nation's need for locomotives. Although even British and American railroads occasionally imported a state-of-the-art locomotive, Italy imported about 386 of the 426 locomotives it had in service between 1839 and 1860.

THE REVOLUTION MOVES EAST

Eastern Europe retained an almost **feudal** society in which many members of the ruling class derived their wealth from agriculture and estate management. Many others in the ruling class received their money from rack rents (a rent whose annual value almost equals the value of the property), feudal dues, and a variety of special privileges that came from birth into the nobility. Such "leaders" were not likely to welcome change, and their attitude discouraged outside investment from those countries to the west that had already embarked on the path toward modernization.

> FEUDAL: of the medieval system under which serfs worked on land held by a lord and gave part of their produce to the lord

Turkey (the Ottoman Empire), Russia, and Austria (the Austro-Hungarian Empire) vied for control of southeastern Europe for much of the nineteenth century.

SOUTHEASTERN EUROPE IN 1913

As was the case elsewhere in Europe, during the preindustrial period in eastern Europe home manufacture accounted for a large percentage of industrial output. Rural industries relied on the putting-out system (see Volume 1) in which individuals processed materials at home and competed with urban industries regulated by artisan guilds. In general, among the lower classes a person who had skill and ambition but lacked money found significantly fewer opportunities the farther east he was born.

AUSTRIA

Austria occupied a geographical position in the center of Europe. Within its boundaries lay the intersections of the west-east and north-south economic divides. Northern and western parts of Austria participated in the opening phases of the Industrial Revolution that spread from England to western Europe. Southern and eastern Austria, by far the larger area, maintained a preindustrial economy based on agriculture.

A water-powered sawmill in rural Austro-Hungary in 1890. In eastern Europe water-powered production continued to exceed steam-powered production.

29

Like Italy, the Napoleonic Wars ravaged Austria. Indeed, along with Great Britain, Austria proved to be Napoleon's most stubborn enemy. The Austrian Empire that emerged after 1815 had the second largest geographic area and third largest population in Europe. It had a complex mix of religions, ethnic groups, and cultures made up of eleven different peoples. A ruling **dynasty**, the Hapsburg family line, held the different peoples together. The story of Austria's Industrial Revolution is one of economic growth in a multicultural setting.

After 1815 the Hapsburg government tried to stimulate modernization through economic and social reform. Those efforts had mixed success. On the economic front western Austria continued to advance, aided by the import of both knowledge and skilled technicians from the more developed nations to the west. In addition Austrian entrepreneurs made significant innovations in the iron, sugar, and brewing industries. Western Austria's **infrastructure** improved with new roads and later the construction of the first railroads. Steam engines appeared in the agricultural, industrial, and transportation sectors. In common with most of Europe, the textile industry led the way. By 1841 mechanized textile production accounted for over 40 percent of total industrial output. Meanwhile, the remote and isolated regions of eastern and southern Austria remained rural, backward, and poor.

Social reforms included the emancipation of the peasantry in 1848, the end to the tariff barrier with Hungary in 1851 (the

DYNASTY: a line of rulers who belong to the same family

INFRASTRUCTURE: underlying support, usually referring to the roads and other services provided to a community

A busy street that served as a marketplace in Vienna, capital of Austro-Hungary.

Hapsburg Empire was also called the Dual Monarchy and the Austro-Hungarian Empire because it linked Austria and Hungary), and a host of educational, legal, and banking measures. However, European-wide economic recession, political turmoil, and a series of wars between 1859 and 1866 retarded industrialization. The railroad boom that stimulated so much German industrialization was much weaker in Austria. While the leading industrial nations of western Europe enjoyed robust growth between 1855 and 1870, Austria failed to keep pace. Moreover, economic reform imposed by the government did not address the lack of political freedom, particularly the nationalist aspirations of some of the ethnic groups that made up the Hapsburg Empire.

A stock market crash in 1873 led to a long and painful economic depression. The depression prompted a movement away from economic reform (called economic liberalism) toward greater emphasis on social control imposed by the government. Although Austria enjoyed a second phase of industrial growth in the last decades of the nineteenth century, it failed to address a basic contradiction that had long plagued the empire: a dynastic monarchy trying to retain control of a multinational state during an era of rising nationalist and democratic yearnings. The assassination of the heir to the Austro-Hungarian throne by a Serbian terrorist in Bosnia in 1914 plunged Europe into World War I and saw the final collapse of the Hapsburg Empire.

THE CZECH LANDS

Prior to 1918 the Czech Lands (the modern Czech and Slovak republics)—Bohemia, Moravia, and Silesia—were part of the Hapsburg Empire. Compared to the western areas in the Hapsburg Empire, these provinces were economically backward. They produced agricultural goods, coal, and iron ore and relatively little in the way of manufactured goods. Most manufacture was a result of the traditional putting-out system. Transport costs were high. Few areas could make use of cheap water transportation. Although the empire had begun building railroads in the 1830s, few lines extended into the Czech Lands, and the privately owned railroad companies charged high rates.

The Czech Lands enjoyed the advantage, as part of the empire, of sharing a common currency and having access to a common national market. But the general poverty of many regions within the empire limited market demand. What most consumers wanted were simple, cheap products.

Textile manufacture, using locally grown flax and locally

raised sheep, mechanized to meet their demand. During the first phase of the region's Industrial Revolution, 1800 to 1830, mechanization came to cotton and wool spinning and the weaving of woolen fabrics. Czech industry began using steam power in the 1820s.

Thereafter came mechanization and factory organization of the food-processing industries, particularly sugar processing, mining, chemical manufacture, and mechanical engineering. Modernization took place last in the iron metallurgy industry and was not completed until about 1880. During the 1870s the major railway lines were completed, and subsequent work focused on building local lines. As was the case elsewhere, railroad construction stimulated industrial development, particularly in the mining, iron metallurgy, and machine-manufacturing industries.

The development of railroads was essential to the growth of coal mining.

Serfdom in Russia:
See also page 51

Steam power could be put to work in any region. Therefore the nearby availability of mineral fuels and the presence of railroads influenced where capitalists established their steam-powered factories. Entire industrial centers arose, some in traditional locations like Prague and others in formerly rural regions. Largely as a consequence of industrialization, Prague's population climbed from 121,000 people in 1843 to 356,000 in 1880 and 566,000 in 1900.

By 1891, Moravia and Silesia employed 85,377 textile workers. Ten years later the number had climbed to 129,730 textile workers, yet nearly half still worked in their homes under the putting-out system. Within the textile industry and elsewhere the Czech Lands lagged behind more modern western European countries. Nonetheless, the Industrial Revolution had caused wide-ranging population shifts from rural to industrial regions that laid the basis for the rise of a modern industrial society.

HUNGARY

Like the Czech Lands, Hungary was part of the Hapsburg Empire (also called the Dual Monarchy because it linked Austria and Hungary). During the years the Industrial Revolution was sweeping through England and western Europe, Hungary remained a rural backwater dominated by a hereditary nobility whose goal was to preserve things the way they were (the status quo). The Revolution of 1848 ended serfdom and many noble privileges. The revolution created the foundation for economic development, but that development was slow in coming. One reason was that the lower nobility still clung to too many powers. In addition, people were used to central control from Vienna, and its absence caused unsettling political problems.

But the Industrial Revolution in the west had two major effects that brought change to Hungary. The west had a growing appetite for agricultural products and raw materials, and Hungary could provide them. In order to move products efficiently, Hungary needed to improve its transportation system. Beginning in 1849, Hungary began building a rail net that dramatically increased trade between Hungary and its neighbors while stimulating Hungarian industry.

Even after the Revolution of 1848 the Hungarian aristocracy owned most of the land, with one percent of all landowners possessing 47.7 percent of the country's total land area. The landowners recognized the opportunity to export agricultural goods to the west. They also understood that they had to modernize in order to fulfill that potential. They were fortunate that both Hungarian banks and foreign investors, particularly German and French, were willing and able to supply credit. Between 1867 and 1900 mortgage loans increased elevenfold.

Landowners used the loans to buy better tools and animal-driven equipment such as seed drills, reapers, and harvesters. The introduction of steam-powered threshing machines led to dramatic increases in farm yields. In 1871 Hungary had about 2,500 such machines. In 1914 the number had increased to 30,000. Along with the agricultural machines came modern crop rotation practices and more intensive cultivation with artificial fertilizers. The results were spectacular: The average yields of wheat, corn, rye, and potatoes increased by 66 percent, 60 percent, 71 percent, and 160 percent respectively.

Hungary's booming export trade had valuable spillover effects. In the 1860s capitalists began building grain-processing mills. It was more profitable to export processed food instead of raw grain, and Hungary became one of the few, if not the only, European country that was able to make the change from exporting raw grain to exporting food products. By 1867, 14 large flour mills operated in Budapest alone. Budapest's milling capacity increased rapidly to the point that the city was second in the world, behind only Minneapolis, Minnesota.

The profit to be made in agriculture, particularly in flour milling, attracted inventors and engineers. As a result, the Hungarian engineering industry took off. Modern engineering practices and mechanization spread to food-processing industries such as sugar refineries. Simultaneously, the expansion of the Hungarian railway system led to the development of a huge iron and steel industry.

Steam power, the spread of machinery, and the development of large-scale mechanized industry created a growing class of industrial workers. Still, as late as 1875, three-quarters of all Hungarian workers labored in the agricultural sector. But their status had changed from serfs to wage earners, and that change, along with the increase in factory

Electric power generators built in Hungary and exported to Russia during the early 1900s.

34

NEVER-ENDING WARFARE AND SHIFTING ALLIANCES

Europe, particularly the nations of southern and eastern Europe, enjoyed neither peace nor independence during the years of industrial growth in western Europe. Napoleon's imperial ambitions sent the armies of France marching across the map of Europe until his final defeat in 1815. The soil of the Netherlands, Prussia, Austro-Hungary, Spain, Italy, and even Russia knew the imprint of French boots. Sweden fought both for and against France and Russia. When the French tide receded, former allies against Napoleon fell into war with one another. Within nations rival factions vied for power and plunged their people into revolution and civil war.

Belgium fought for and won independence from the Netherlands from 1830 to 1832. Spain fought internal wars from 1834 to 1839 and again from 1840 to 1843. Italy endured revolutions in 1821 and again in 1831, and occupation by Austro-Hungary in 1847. It fought for independence the following year, but lost. Decades of war finally resulted in Italy becoming a unified nation in 1870. Greece fought wars from 1821 to 1832, in 1862, 1878, and again in 1896. Hungary fought for independence from Austria in 1848 but failed.

No sooner had Russia repulsed Napoleon's army than it went to war with Persia (1821-1823) and Turkey (1828-1829). The Ottoman Empire of Turkey fought Russia for control of the Balkan region. Turning eastward, Russia fought to annex territory in Central Asia between 1839 and 1847, and again from 1864 to 1876 and 1884 to 1885. Russia's most costly conflict was the Crimean War (1853-1856). Russia occupied Turkey's Balkan possessions, and France and Great Britain intervened on Turkey's side. Half a million people died in that war, most of them from disease.

Such expenditures of blood and treasure robbed Europe of its wealth. The burden of near-constant warfare fell most heavily on the poorest peoples.

Top: Napoleon defeated Austria in 1809 and claimed the Kaiser's daughter as his bride.

Above: Archduke Karl, the brother of the kaiser (Austria's Hapsburg monarch), led the Austrian army against Napoleon's forces in 1809.

Left: The major campaign of the Crimean War was the siege of Sevastopol, Russia's naval base on the Black Sea. The Russians held out for nearly a year, and the final battle for Sevastopol cost a total of 23,000 lives.

Compared to England, Bulgaria had longer and colder winters. Consequently woolens were more popular than cotton fabrics. Also, the Turkish army had first choice of most nonwoolen fabrics for soldiers' uniforms. So when the Industrial Revolution came to Bulgaria, the first machines were used for woolen manufacture.

The year 1834 saw the construction of Bulgaria's first woolen textile factory in Sliven. That was only about 30 years after the appearance of the first woolen textile factories in England and actually occurred before such a factory had been built in France. Still, the factory lagged behind the standards of mechanization set in England. The crude spinning machines came from Russia. Rather than spend scarce money on imported machinery, local ironmasters copied the crude Russian design. Nonetheless, the Sliven factory was a tremendous advance by Bulgarian standards, so the Ottoman rulers seized control and operated it for the benefit of the Turkish army. It expanded considerably during the 1840s and was completely rebuilt with new English equipment during the next two decades. The success of the Sliven factory led to the establishment of a few other woolen factories. However, as late as 1877 handicraft production far exceeded the machine production of woolen textiles.

Bulgarian peasants—shown here in 1923—supplied raw wool, but their lives remained unchanged by their nation's growing woolen industry.

In 1877 war broke out between Turkey and Russia. During the 15 years preceding that war, a small number of additional factories had begun operation, including seven steam-powered mills, two large silk factories, a state-owned printing establishment, two small soap factories, a shoe polish factory, and a small factory that produced macaroni and vermicelli. As this lists suggests, factory production had not advanced very far on the eve of war. Some 25 industrial facilities that could be counted as factories employed no more than about 760 workers, only 0.1 percent of the total work force. When war came, military operations and the associated destruction and pillage wrecked many of Bulgaria's industrial sites.

The war brought Bulgarian independence from Turkish rule and launched a period of industrial expansion. Thirty-six large steam and water mills were operating in Bulgaria by 1887 along with five textile factories, eight leather-processing plants, five distilleries, ten breweries, three soap factories, one cement factory, and one dyeing plant. Over a 17-year period that represented almost a 9 percent annual growth in industrial enterprise, although it is important to remember that Bulgaria was beginning from a very small industrial base.

New government initiatives in the second half of the 1890s led to accelerated industrial growth. The government raised

Bulgaria: The Establishment of New Large Industrial Enterprises

1880–1884	23
1885–1889	33
1890–1894	54

Latecomers to the Industrial Revolution initially had to rely on copies of obsolete machinery to equip their early factories.

import duties to protect the young industries against more mature foreign competition while at the same time creating incentives to encourage domestic industry. A reduction in interest rates caused investors to take money out of banks and instead channel it into industry. As a result of those initiatives, the number of large industrial facilities rose from 72 in 1894 to 389 in 1912. Again came conflict to interrupt industrial development as Bulgaria experienced three wars between 1912 and 1923 followed by an economic crisis.

On the eve of the first Balkan War in 1912 Bulgaria was enjoying industrial growth rates that rivaled the fastest rates experienced by western Europe and the United States. Yet traditional handicraft production still accounted for up to half of all manufacture in a variety of sectors, including metal goods, shoes, clothing, millinery, and baking. It is estimated that in 1912 handicraft workers outnumbered factory workers by at least six to one.

ROMANIA

The lack of reliable data makes it difficult to say precisely when and to what extent the Industrial Revolution arrived in Romania. What is certain is that two key developments occurred in the 1870s that greatly stimulated industrial

Local laborers were hired to do the dirtiest jobs at foreign-owned industrial facilities in eastern Europe. Romanian workers clean up waste at an American-owned petroleum plant in 1923.

Romania: The Establishment of New Large Industrial Enterprises	
1866	39
1879	87
1887	171
1904	471

Ammunition factories of the 1880s on the Greek island of Crete.

development. In 1875 the government established the first protectionist duty to shelter emerging industry from more mature foreign competition. The Bank of Bucharest also was founded around that time, and it provided the financial resources for capitalists to create industrial facilities.

Bucharest, the capital, was the center of early industrial development. It featured a railway depot, two large sugar refineries, and seven steam mills. After 1887 either the state or private capitalists created an average of 19 new large industrial facilities per year. At first most of them were in the textile or food-processing sectors (milling, distilling, brewing). The twentieth century witnessed the rise of metalworking and chemical manufacture. In addition, Romania's oil fields experienced rapid development, mostly caused by foreign investment.

Compared to Bulgaria, Romania had a more diversified industrial base. It also saw factory manufacture more quickly replace handicraft manufacture. By 1902 total factory production exceeded artisan manufacture. Nonetheless, like Bulgaria, Romania's handicraft manufacturing sector remained important long past the time such manufacture had declined in the more industrialized West. Also like Bulgaria, Romanian development suffered when the country became involved in World War I (1914-1918).

BALKAN SUMMARY

Compared to the advanced capitalist western countries, the Balkan nations were backwards. This delayed both the arrival and the spread of Balkan industrialization. In each Balkan country someone, either the state or private capitalists or the combination of the two, tried to import the West's inventions and innovations. But industrialization thrives only when certain conditions are met, and in the Balkans those isolated efforts failed to stimulate national industrial growth until late in the nineteenth century. The first substantial phase of industrialization came to Romania, Croatia, and Slovenia in the 1860s. Industrialization came to Serbia after 20 more years and to Bulgaria, Greece, and Bosnia-Hercegovina during the 1890s.

Still, none of the Balkan countries matched the "first comers" in per capita (per person) industrial output during their Industrial Revolutions. Even by the beginning of World

Serbia: The Establishment of New Large Industrial Enterprises	
1898	28
1902	66
1906	110
1910	428

War II (1939-1945) the Balkan countries had not reached the economic level of advanced capitalist nations. Because the nations of southeast Europe lagged so far behind the west, historians remain divided over the question of whether that region ever experienced an industrial revolution.

Industrialization and mechanization had not yet come to Bosnia. Farmers stuck to age-old practices for tasks such as threshing. Even in 1890 farmers used flails or horses (left) to separate grain from the stalks and husks.

THE SLOW GROWTH OF AN INDUSTRIAL GIANT

Empress Catherine II assumed power in Russia in 1762. At that time Russia stood high on the list of great economic powers by virtue of its numerous factories and workshops, volume of production, and role in European trade. One hundred years later, a span of time encompassing the birth and spread of the Industrial Revolution, Russia had lost its high economic rank.

The Russian decline occurred for a number of reasons. Geographically, Russia was distant from Europe's great trade routes. It was a huge land without a developed road network,

Peter I (called Peter the Great), czar of Russia from 1682 to 1725, toured England for fifteen months in 1697 and 1698. "His whole impression, as derived from his fifteen months' tour, must have been a noisy, vast, smoky vista of factories, foundries, shipyards, wharves and machinery." After his tour, Peter tried to introduce western technology to Russia.

Catherine II (later known as Catherine the Great) was a German who was unhappily married to a German-born grandson of Peter the Great. She became empress of Russia in 1762 by leading troops to oust her husband, who had just taken the throne as Peter III. She ruled until her death in 1796.

Typical of the early 1800s in Russia, people on the lowest rungs of the economic ladder moved freight by dragging loaded sleds though the snow.

had a harsh climate and an underdeveloped agricultural sector, and suffered from periodic famines. Its peasant masses had a low standard of living, and its middle class was small and insignificant. But the foremost problem hampering economic development was its ruling class, which resisted change while upholding the supremacy of the landowning class. For all of these reasons Russia stagnated during the first half of the nineteenth century and did not share in the revolution that transformed western economies.

RUSSIA AT MIDCENTURY

As was the case in most of Europe, Russia's textile industry

Russia's first spinning mill began operation in Moscow in 1808. When Moscow burned in 1812 during the Napoleonic Wars, the city's textile industry came to a halt. However, by 1843 Russia had about 350,000 spindles in operation. Yet in the early 1900s some peasants still spun with a single hand-held spindle, (hanging from the woman's right hand) without the aid of even a spinning wheel.

Coke smelting:
See also
Volume 2 page 35

was the first to experience widespread mechanization. In the 1840s the number of spindles in use (a good measure of mechanization) in the cotton industry began to rise dramatically. Yet steam power was uncommon. Likewise, the level of use of mechanical looms in the woolen industry was low, with wool weaving and much else remaining an artisan industry.

Unlike in England, mechanization remained largely confined within the cotton industry. Other innovations were likewise scarce. For example, in the iron industry smelters mostly used charcoal—which did not produce as much heat as coke—for smelting as late as 1861. Only about 12 percent of the power

In 1800 Russia was the foremost producer of pig iron, but by 1860 it hardly exceeded tiny Belgium's production. In manufactured iron it had fallen to eighth place behind Austria. Even as late as the early 1900s, smelting was still largely fueled by charcoal. Russian woodcutters posed before the great pile of wood they cut for smelting iron ore.

Opposite: Empress Catherine II abandoned her plans to free the serfs when she realized it would be politically unpopular among the aristocrats who supported her. In 1815 the economic adviser to Czar Alexander I (Catherine's grandson) observed that "the superiority of free labor over serf labor is even more apparent in industry than in agriculture." However, Russia did not free its serfs until 1861. Once the serfs gained their freedom, many continued to farm using ancient hand tools.

Below: An enormous gulf continued to exist between the cottages of farm laborers and the mansions of aristocrats.

used came from steam engines, while water-powered turbines provided the balance. Russia imported most of the machines it used and had not developed many machine tool or engineering workshops. Because it was based on imported machinery, the mechanization of the cotton industry neither stimulated progress in other industries nor changed Russia's economy and social structure.

The key social development that launched Russia's Industrial Revolution came in 1861 with the Emancipation Act, which freed the serfs (people in feudal servitude, bound to their master's land and transferred with the land when it passed to another owner). The act gave freedom of movement to millions of peasants and ultimately provided a large labor pool for industry to recruit.

After midcentury Russia began an exceptional rate of population increase, rising from 68 million in 1858 to 163 million in 1914 (both figures exclude Finland and Poland, which Russia occupied during that period). At the same time, agricultural production steadily increased. Russia was able to

feed its own population, as long as the harvest was decent, and even to export crops like wheat and barley. In addition, the agricultural sector provided raw materials like cotton, tobacco, leather, and sugar to the industrial sector. Labor productivity improved, which meant that workers were available to enter newly created industries.

Still Russia was a backward and poor country, with per capita income among the lowest in Europe. A very small percentage of the aristocratic rich enjoyed a lavish lifestyle. Each year they alone purchased so many luxuries that it amounted to 10 percent of the imports for the entire nation. Most of the population depended on the size of each harvest to prosper. When crops failed, famine came.

Nonetheless, Russia's expanding agricultural sector led to a gradual rise in average incomes, since most of the Russian economy remained agricultural. A growing population with more money created a growing demand that stimulated industrial development.

Once the serfs gained their freedom, many continued to live in rural villages.

Foreigners built many of Russia's early rail lines, locomotives, and train cars. For example, Americans built the entire Moscow-St. Petersburg rail line, which opened in 1854, as well as 162 locomotives and 2,700 freight and passenger cars. The existence of a rail line conferred great advantage to any town or region hoping to expand its industry.

INDUSTRIALIZATION TAKES OFF

Russia's Industrial Revolution took off in the 1870s, propelled by the railways and associated advances in engineering and metallurgy. Railroad construction played an essential part in industrialization by creating demand for new products, such as rails and locomotives, and by linking the nation's geographically vast domestic market. During the first railroad boom in the 1870s most construction took place in western, or European, Russia. Imports supplied the locomotives and most of the pig iron, steel, and machinery.

The second boom in the 1890s was more closely tied to

Smelters at a Russian copper works.

FUELING INDUSTRIAL GROWTH

Industrial production had long been powered by water, wood, or charcoal. Coal-fired steam engines took over as the power source for industry, and most factories run by the old sources of power could no longer compete. Manufacturers had once located their factories along rivers and their furnaces near forests. As coal use expanded, manufacturers established factories in coal-mining regions. In eastern Europe and Russia the regions endowed with coal deposits were the first to industrialize. Then as railroads expanded during the late 1800s, trains carried coal to other regions and promoted the spread of industry.

By making coal widely available, railroads promoted the growth of industry, and expanding industry in turn created a higher demand for coal. The growth of the Russian iron and steel industry during the late 1800s serves as an example. The largely agricultural Ukraine in southern Russia possessed rich deposits of both iron and coal. Beginning in the 1870s, coal fueled the growth of the iron industry in the region. Coal provided fuel not only for the blast furnaces but also for locomotives to haul the pig iron to market. Between 1860 and 1900 Russia's railroad network grew from barely 1,000 miles of track to more than 29,000 miles, and Russian factories built 8,000 locomotives. The annual output of coal mines increased from less than half a million to 16 million tons, and that of the iron and steel industry grew from less than half a million to more than five million tons.

GROWTH OF RUSSIAN COAL AND IRON & STEEL PRODUCTION

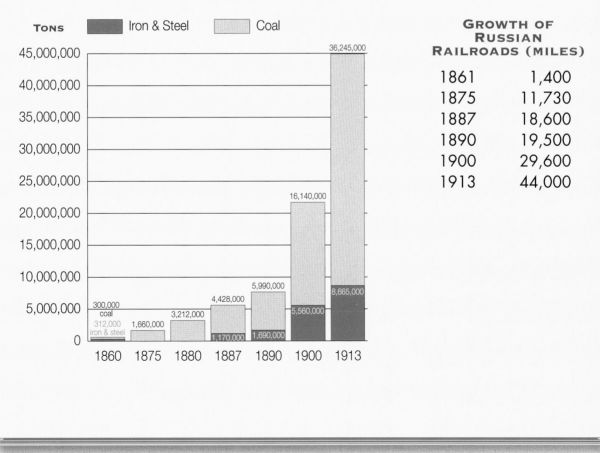

GROWTH OF RUSSIAN RAILROADS (MILES)	
1861	1,400
1875	11,730
1887	18,600
1890	19,500
1900	29,600
1913	44,000

emerging heavy industries, including modern steel production. Construction in the 1890s linked natural resources, particularly iron and coal, with manufacturing centers. Belgian and French investors and engineers led the way by developing coal mines in southern Ukraine. English entrepreneurs established iron works and engineering plants that made precision tools. French capital backed the exploitation of iron ore. German capitalists oversaw the installation of state-of-the-art steel mills and modern engineering facilities. A traveler observed that the factories in Ukraine were practically identical to those in Germany.

An open hearth furnace at a Russian steel works. Compared to other nations, Russian factories operated on a huge scale. Around 1910 more than one-third of Russian industrial workers labored in facilities that employed more than 500 people.

As the twentieth century began, Russia was a major industrial power. However, the social transformations that accompanied the Industrial Revolution elsewhere had not occurred in Russia. In 1913 more than three million people were working in factories and mines, but they represented a small percentage of the total work force of some 50 million. The overwhelming majority of Russians continued to labor in the agricultural sector. Agricultural products made up three-quarters of all export earnings.

The putting-out system of home manufacture continued to make a large contribution to industrial output. Urban craftsmen and, more importantly, rural peasant households toiled with their hand tools during the winter before returning to the fields in the spring, just as they had in preindustrial times. Such cottage industry met a large percentage of domestic consumer demand. Peasant handicrafts provided over one-third of industrial production in 1913.

The Russian government played a much greater role in the nation's economic life than did governments in western Europe and the United States. The government provided subsidies, loans, land grants, tax relief, and even exemption from military duty in order to encourage selected entrepreneurs. However, it was interested neither in promoting capitalism nor in allowing genuine economic freedom. Instead, its economic goal was to strengthen the position of the government. For example, while

Cottage industry:
See also
Volume 1 pages 31–33

The textile industry experienced the type of modernization and expansion that had occurred elsewhere. Between 1861 and 1880 cotton production increased 400 percent. As a result, machine-made cottons largely replaced the traditional linens made by cottage workers. A new cotton mill under construction in Russia, early 1900s.

other major governments imposed tariffs to protect developing industries, the Russian government relied on tariffs as a revenue source. The government set the highest tariffs in all of Europe, and as a result, customs receipts accounted for about one-third of state revenue.

The high tariffs had several negative economic consequences. They increased costs for imported raw materials, machinery, and spare parts, thus discouraging investment. By acting as a barrier against innovation, the tariffs protected inefficient domestic industries and promoted monopolies. Around the beginning of the twentieth century some of Russia's most powerful cartels (associations between financial or industrial interests in order to make a monopoly) formed, most notably in the steel and coal-mining sectors.

The state bureaucracy seemed to work against foreign investment. Foreigners had to deal with multiple layers of a corrupt bureaucracy and often had to use bribes to remain in business. Yet the sheer size of the Russian market and its potential for profit continued to attract foreign investment. In the 1880s about 41 percent of new industrial investment

Russian peasants continued to bring their farm produce and handicrafts to sell in towns. A St. Petersburg street market.

Oil industry:
See also
Volume 8 pages 26–31

Estimated Capacity of All Steam Engines (in thousands of horsepower)

	1840	1850	1860	1870	1880
Great Britain	620	1,290	2,450	4,400	7,600
Belgium	40	70	160	350	610
France	90	270	1,120	1,850	3,070
Germany	40	260	850	2,480	5,120
Netherlands	0	10	30	130	250
Austria	20	100	330	800	1,560
Italy	10	40	50	330	500
Spain	10	20	100	210	470
Sweden	0	0	20	100	220
Russia	20	70	200	920	1,740
Europe total	**860**	**2,240**	**5,540**	**11,570**	**22,000**
United States	**760**	**1,680**	**3,470**	**5,590**	**9,110**
World	**1,650**	**3,990**	**9,380**	**18,460**	**34,150**

RUSSIAN OIL

Russian capitalists had long been aware that oil existed at Baku, in the Caucasus Mountains, but few had been willing to spend the money to extract and transport it. Russian entrepreneurs began pumping small amounts of crude oil around 1865. By the 1880s oil pipelines and railroad tanker cars were serving the region. Within a decade crude oil production had increased more than tenfold because the improved transportation attracted foreign investment. Russians used some oil for lighting and as locomotive fuel, but most petroleum products were exported. By 1891 Russian exports of kerosene met 30 percent of world demand. Around 1900 Russia pumped half the world's crude oil, but a decade later only a quarter of the world's oil came from Russia. Russia's share of world production fell for two reasons: the rapid growth of oil production in America, and heavy taxation imposed on oil production by the Russian government.

RUSSIAN CRUDE OIL PRODUCTION (IN TONS):

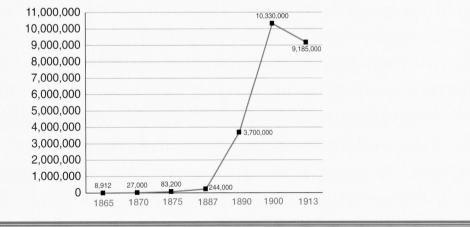

came from from outside of Russia. Between 1903 and 1905 this figure rose to 87 percent. Foreign nations each tried to find a special niche, with German companies emphasizing chemical and electrical industries, French investing in metallurgy and engineering, and British helping develop the oil industry.

Overall, western and particularly German entrepreneurs invested so heavily in Russian industrialization that by 1910 foreign capital accounted for about half of the capital invested in Russian companies. On the eve of World War I Russia carried the heaviest debt load in Europe.

Technology transfer from from abroad matched the influx of capital. Bell (USA) and Ericsson (Sweden) introduced telephones; Siemens (Germany) established the manufacture of telegraphic equipment; International Harvester (USA) developed agricultural machine industry; Singer (USA) brought the sewing machine. Because Russia practically imported entire industries, the country had little incentive to develop its own technicians.

Increasing industrialization brought with it the familiar pattern of long work days, squalid working and living conditions, and workers' protests. The **czarist** government proved no more tolerant than any other European government

CZARIST: in Russian history the period of rule by monarchs called czars

TECHNOLOGY TRANSFER: the movement of techniques and devices from one place to another

By 1913 Russia had become the largest wheat exporter in the world. Agriculture provided three-quarters of Russian exports, and the overwhelming number of Russian workers labored in the agricultural sector. A few large farms were able to afford McCormick reapers from America.

and squashed such protests. At the same time, factory owners and managers routinely ignored the Factory Acts, which were introduced in the 1880s in an effort to improve working conditions.

Russia had joined the ranks of the major industrial powers by 1914. Its industrial output placed it fourth in the world behind the United States, the United Kingdom, and Germany. But the czarist government displayed a woeful inability to change with the times. Industrial development had not caused a social transformation in a state where the majority of people looked forward to a brighter future. Instead, ahead lay ruinous war, revolution, and communist rule. Joseph Stalin used the power of his police state to force Russia through an intense period of industrialization between the world wars. His successors did the same after the end of World War II in 1945.

From the beginning of the Industrial Revolution very little in Russian society encouraged the spirit of enterprise. Rather than have a competitive market economy dictate economic development, the government imposed industrialization from the top. The consequences of this history are still felt today in the modern world.

Joseph Stalin's first "five-year plan" began in 1928. It brought about Russia's second Industrial Revolution at a huge cost in lives and freedom.

PRODUCTION AND DESTRUCTION: THE WORLD WARS

Although the wars of the nineteenth century had robbed nations of their wealth and people, twentieth century wars proved even more costly and destructive. Nations threw all their manpower, resources, technology, and industrial capacity into the task of destroying their enemies. Steel went to build weapons and machines of destruction. In World War I (1914-1918) scientists formulated chemicals to poison and to blast enemy soldiers. In World War II (1939-1945) chemical explosives destroyed enemy factories and reduced entire cities to rubble. A nation's soldiers took priority in the distribution of food and clothing. The need for soldiers to hurl themselves against the enemy took priority over the need for agricultural and industrial workers. All of this was enormously costly from an economic standpoint. The warring nations spent some $280 billion to fight World War I and more than one and a half trillion dollars to fight World War II. At the end of each war the victors redrew the map of Europe, and the defeated struggled to rebuild their shattered economies.

No nation suffered more from the two world wars than Russia. In March 1917, in the midst of World War I, Russia erupted in revolution. Workers, mired in poverty, sought to end the monopoly of the upper classes on wealth and power. Worker protests and military mutinies forced the czar from power. Soldiers and sailors murdered their officers, the Russian military fell apart, and Russia descended into chaos. A few months later a second revolution placed Vladimir Lenin and the Communists in control of Russia.

When World War I ended, more than 14 million soldiers and civilians had died, including three million Russians. The victors imposed new conditions: Austria lost control of its empire, and Czechoslovakia and Hungary became independent nations; Germany struggled to pay huge sums demanded as reparations, and the resulting hardship induced Germans to elevate Adolph Hitler to power in 1933, leading to World War II.

Russian infantrymen in World War I endured squalid conditions in the trenches.

A workers' demonstration in Petrograd, Russia, in 1917. The banners proclaim "Down with Ministers and Capitalists! All Power to the Soviets!"

Russia, meanwhile, remained in a state of war until 1922 as various groups tried to unseat Lenin's Communist government. Russia lost a significant portion of its industrial capacity during the long years of war, revolution, and civil war. In addition, Russia's enormous loss of life depleted the workforce for years to come. Moreover, foreign nations were reluctant to trade with the Communists, depriving them of the ability to import the machinery and materials required by Russia's factories.

Because of war and revolution Russia fell behind in the great race to industrialize. Russia's new leadership ruthlessly drove the country to complete its industrial revolution.

The world again plunged into total war in 1939, when Hitler's armies began invading Germany's neighboring countries. Initially Russia allied itself with Germany, but Germany turned against its ally in 1941, forcing Russia to ally with Great Britain and, later, the United States.

The Industrial Revolution had provided the world with unprecedented productive power: Advances in science and industry were now turned to the task of making destruction more efficient. One hundred million troops fought World War II, and 15 million of them died in combat. Between 26 and 34 million civilians died, of disease or starvation, in concentration camps or in cities destroyed by enemy bombs. Russia paid dearly for victory with the lives of at least 20 million of its people.

After Germany's defeat Russia shared in the victors' privilege of redrawing the map. As a result, part of Germany and most of Eastern Europe—including Bulgaria, Czechoslovakia (composed of Bohemia, Moravia, and Slovakia), Hungary, Romania, and Yugoslavia (composed of Bosnia, Croatia, Macedonia, Serbia, and Slovenia)—fell under communist control, where they remained through 1989.

Most of these nations had been "latecomers" to the Industrial Revolution. World War II caused them to fall farther behind. In an effort to catch up, the leaders of the Communist Party imposed central planning on industrialization in the Soviet Union, and all the nations under Communist control followed suit. The workers who had fought for communism in 1917 had hoped for worker ownership and control of the means of production. The reality of Communism in power was that the central government—supposedly representing the workers—controlled everything. Communism proved unable to compete economically with the rest of the industrialized world.

A DATELINE OF MAJOR EVENTS DURING THE INDUSTRIAL REVOLUTION

BEFORE 1750	1760	1770	1780

REVOLUTIONS IN INDUSTRY AND TECHNOLOGY

1619: English settlers establish the first iron works in colonial America, near Jamestown, Virginia.

1689: Thomas Savery (England) patents the first design for a steam engine.

1709: Englishman Abraham Darby uses coke instead of coal to fuel his blast furnace.

1712: Englishman Thomas Newcomen builds the first working steam engine.

1717: Thomas Lombe establishes a silk-throwing factory in England.

1720: The first Newcomen steam engine on the Continent is installed at a Belgian coal mine.

1733: James Kay (England) invents the flying shuttle.

1742: Benjamin Huntsman begins making crucible steel in England.

1756: The first American coal mine opens.

1764: In England James Hargreaves invents the spinning jenny.

1769: Englishman Richard Arkwright patents his spinning machine, called a water frame.

James Watt of Scotland patents an improved steam engine design.

Josiah Wedgwood (England) opens his Etruria pottery works.

1771: An industrial spy smuggles drawings of the spinning jenny from England to France.

1774: John Wilkinson (England) builds machines for boring cannon cylinders.

1775: Arkwright patents carding, drawing, and roving machines.

In an attempt to end dependence on British textiles American revolutionaries open a spinning mill in Philadelphia using a smuggled spinning-jenny design.

1777: Oliver Evans (U.S.) invents a card-making machine.

1778: John Smeaton (England) introduces cast iron gearing to transfer power from waterwheels to machinery.

The water closet (indoor toilet) is invented in England.

1779: Englishman Samuel Crompton develops the spinning mule.

1783: Englishman Thomas Bell invents a copper cylinder to print patterns on fabrics.

1784: Englishman Henry Cort invents improved rollers for rolling mills and the puddling process for refining pig iron.

Frenchman Claude Berthollet discovers that chlorine can be used as a bleach.

The ironworks at Le Creusot use France's first rotary steam engine to power its hammers, as well as using the Continent's first coke-fired blast furnace.

1785: Englishman Edmund Cartwright invents the power loom.

1788: The first steam engine is imported into Germany.

REVOLUTIONS IN TRANSPORTATION AND COMMUNICATION

1757: The first canal is built in England.

1785: The first canal is built in the United States, at Richmond, Virginia.

1787: John Fitch and James Rumsey (U.S.) each succeed in launching a working steamboat.

Locks on an English canal

SOCIAL REVOLUTIONS

1723: Britain passes an act to allow the establishment of workhouses for the poor.

1750: The enclosure of common land gains momentum in Britain.

1776: Scottish professor Adam Smith publishes *The Wealth of Nations*, which promotes laissez-faire capitalism.

The workhouse

INTERNATIONAL RELATIONS

1775–1783: The American Revolution. Thirteen colonies win their independence from Great Britain and form a new nation, the United States of America.

1789–1793: The French Revolution leads to abolition of the monarchy and execution of the king and queen. Mass executions follow during the Reign of Terror, 1793–1794.

Continental Army in winter quarters at Valley Forge

1790	1800	1810	1820
1790: English textile producer Samuel Slater begins setting up America's first successful textile factory in Pawtucket, Rhode Island. Jacob Perkins (U.S.) invents a machine capable of mass-producing nails. **1791:** French chemist Nicholas Leblanc invents a soda-making process. **1793:** Eli Whitney (U.S.) invents a cotton gin. **1794:** Germany's first coke-fired blast furnace is built. The first German cotton spinning mill installs Arkwright's water frame. **1798:** Eli Whitney devises a system for using power-driven machinery to produce interchangeable parts, the model for the "American System" of manufacture. Wool-spinning mills are built in Belgium using machinery smuggled out of England. A cylindrical papermaking machine is invented in England.	**1801:** American inventor Oliver Evans builds the first working high-pressure steam engine and uses it to power a mill. Joseph-Marie Jacquard (France) invents a loom that uses punch cards to produce patterned fabrics. A cotton-spinning factory based on British machinery opens in Belgium. The first cotton-spinning mill in Switzerland begins operation. Austria establishes the Continent's largest cotton-spinning mill. **1802:** In England William Murdock uses coal gas to light an entire factory. Richard Trevithick builds a high-pressure steam engine in England. **1807:** British businessmen open an industrial complex in Belgium that includes machine manufacture, coal mining, and iron production. **1808:** Russia's first spinning mill begins production in Moscow.	**1810:** Henry Maudslay (England) invents the precision lathe. **1816:** Steam power is used for the first time in an American paper mill. English scientist Humphry Davy invents a safety lamp for coal miners in England. **1817:** The French iron industry's first puddling works and rolling mills are established. **1819:** Thomas Blanchard (U.S.) invents a gunstock-turning lathe, which permits production of standardized parts. 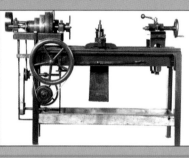 A turning lathe	**1821:** Massachusetts businessmen begin developing Lowell as a site for textile mills. **1822:** Power looms are introduced in French factories. **1820s:** Spinning mills begin operation in Sweden. Steam power is first used in Czech industry. **1827:** A water-driven turbine is invented in France.
1794: The 66-mile Philadelphia and Lancaster turnpike begins operation.  Along an American Highway	**1802:** In England Richard Trevithick builds his first steam locomotive. **1807:** Robert Fulton launches the Clermont, the first commercially successful steamboat, on the Hudson River in New York.	**1811:** Robert Fulton and his partner launch the first steamboat on the Mississippi River. Construction begins on the Cumberland Road (later renamed the National Road) from Baltimore, Maryland, to Wheeling, Virginia. **1815:** In England John McAdam develops an improved technique for surfacing roads. **1819:** The first steamship crosses the Atlantic Ocean.	**1825:** The 363-mile Erie Canal is completed in America. In England the first passenger railroad, the Stockton and Darlington Railway, begins operation. **1826:** The 2-mile horse-drawn Granite Railroad in Massachusetts becomes the first American railroad.
1790: First American patent law passed. Philadelphia begins building a public water system. **1798:** Robert Owen takes over the New Lanark mills and begins implementing his progressive ideas.	**1800:** Parliament prohibits most labor union activity. **1802:** Parliament passes a law limiting the working hours of poor children and orphans.	**1811–1816:** Luddite rioters destroy textile machinery in England. **1819:** Parliament extends legal protection to all child laborers. British cavalry fire at demonstrators demanding voting reform in Manchester, killing 11 and wounding hundreds, including women and children.	**1827:** Carpenters organize the first national trade union in Britain. 
1799: Napoleon Bonaparte seizes control of France's government. **1792–1815:** The Napoleonic Wars involve most of Europe, Great Britain, and Russia. France occupies many of its neighboring nations, reorganizes their governments, and changes their borders.		**1812–1815:** War between the United States and Great Britain disrupts America's foreign trade and spurs the development of American industry.	18th–century carpenter

A DATELINE OF MAJOR EVENTS DURING THE INDUSTRIAL REVOLUTION

	1830	1840	1850	1860
REVOLUTIONS IN INDUSTRY AND TECHNOLOGY	1830: Switzerland's first weaving mill established. 1831: British researcher Michael Faraday builds an electric generator. American inventor Cyrus McCormick builds a horse-drawn mechanical reaper. 1834: Bulgaria's first textile factory is built. 1835: Samuel Colt (U.S) invents the Colt revolver. The first steam engine is used to power a paper mill in Croatia. 1836: The first Hungarian steam mill, the Pest Rolling Mill company, begins using steam power to process grain. 1837: The first successful coke-fired blast furnace in the United States begins operation.	American blacksmith John Deere introduces the first steel plow. 1842: Britain lifts restrictions on exporting textile machinery. *Making Bessemer steel*	1849: The California Gold Rush begins. 1850: Swedish sawmills begin using steam power. 1851: The Great Exhibition opens at the Crystal Palace in London. William Kelly of Kentucky invents a process for converting pig iron to steel. 1852: Hydraulic mining is introduced in the American West. 1853: The first cotton-spinning mill opens in India. 1856: William Perkin (England) synthesizes the first coal tar dye. Henry Bessemer (England) announces his process for converting pig iron to steel. Isaac Singer (U.S.) introduces the sewing machine.	1859: Edwin Drake successfully drills for oil in Pennsylvania. 1863: Ernest Solvay of Belgium begins working on a process to recover ammonia from soda ash in order to produce bleaching powder. 1864: Switzerland's first major chemical company is established. The Siemens-Martin open-hearth steelmaking process is perfected in France. 1865: The first oil pipeline opens in America. The rotary web press is invented in America, permitting printing on both sides of the paper. 1866: U.S. government surveyors discover the largest-known deposit of iron ore in the world in the Mesabi Range of northern Minnesota.
REVOLUTIONS IN TRANSPORTATION AND COMMUNICATION	1830: The first locomotive-powered railroad to offer regular service begins operating in South Carolina. The opening of the Liverpool and Manchester Railway marks the beginning of the British railroad boom. 1833: The 60-mile Camden and Amboy Railroad of New Jersey is completed. 1835: Construction begins on Germany's first railroad.	1836: First railroad built in Russia. 1843: Tunnel completed under the Thames River, London, England, the world's first to be bored through soft clay under a riverbed. 1844: Samuel Morse (U.S.) sends the first message via his invention, the telegraph. The nation's first steam-powered sawmill begins operation on the West Coast.	1846: First railroad built in Hungary. 1853: The first railway is completed in India. 1854: Americans complete the Moscow-St. Petersburg railroad line. 1855: Switzerland's first railroad opens.	1859: In France Etienne Lenoir invents an internal combustion engine. 1860–1861: The Pony Express, a system of relay riders, carries mail to and from America's West Coast. 1866: The transatlantic telegraph cable is completed. Congress authorizes construction of a transcontinental telegraph line. 1869: The tracks of two railroad companies meet at Promontory, Utah, to complete America's first transcontinental railroad
SOCIAL REVOLUTIONS	1833: Parliament passes the Factory Act to protect children working in textile factories. 1836–1842: The English Chartist movement demands Parliamentary reform, but its petitions are rejected by Parliament. 1838: The U.S. Congress passes a law regulating steamboat boiler safety, the first attempt by the federal government to regulate private behavior in the interest of public safety.	1842: Parliament bans the employment of children and women underground in mines. 1845: Russia bans strikes. 1847: A new British Factory Act limits working hours to 10 hours a day or 58 hours a week for children aged 13 to 18 and for women. 1848: Marx and Engels coauthor the *Communist Manifesto*.	1854: In England Charles Dickens publishes *Hard Times*, a novel based on his childhood as a factory worker. 1857: Brooklyn, New York, builds a city wastewater system.	1860–1910: More than 20 million Europeans emigrate to the United States. 1866: National Labor Union forms in the United States. 1869: Knights of Labor forms in the United States. Founding of the Great Atlantic and Pacific Tea Company (A&P) in the U.S.
INTERNATIONAL RELATIONS	1839–1842: Great Britain defeats China in a war and forces it to open several ports to trade.	1847: Austro-Hungary occupies Italy. 1848: Failed revolutions take place in France, Germany, and Austro-Hungary. Serfdom ends in Austro-Hungary.	1853: The American naval officer Commodore Matthew Perry arrives in Japan. 1853–1856: France, Britain, and Turkey defeat Russia in the Crimean War. 1858: Great Britain takes control of India, retaining it until 1947.	1861–1865: The American Civil War brings about the end of slavery in the United States and disrupts raw cotton supplies for U.S. and foreign cotton mills. 1867: Britain gains control of parts of Malaysia. Malaysia is a British colony from 1890 to 1957.

1870	1880	1890	1900

1860s: Agricultural machinery introduced in Hungary.

1870: John D. Rockefeller establishes the Standard Oil Company (U.S.).

1873: The Bethlehem Steel Company begins operation in Pennsylvania.

1875: The first modern iron and steel works opens in India.

Investment in the Japan's cotton industry booms.

1876: Philadelphia hosts the Centennial Exposition.

1877: Hungary installs its first electrical system.

1879: Charles Brush builds the nation's first arc-lighting system in San Francisco.

Thomas Edison (U.S.) develops the first practical incandescent light bulb.

1870s: Japan introduces mechanical silk-reeling.

1882: In New York City the Edison Electric Illuminating Company begins operating the world's first centralized electrical generating station.

1884: The U.S. Circuit Court bans hydraulic mining.

George Westinghouse (U.S.) founds Westinghouse Electric Company.

English engineer Charles Parsons develops a steam turbine.

1885: The introduction of band saws makes American lumbering more efficient.

German inventor Carl Benz builds a self-propelled vehicle powered by a single cylinder gas engine with electric ignition.

1887: An English power plant is the first to use steam turbines to generate electricity.

1888: Nikola Tesla (U.S.) invents an

alternating current electric motor.

1894: An American cotton mill becomes the first factory ever built to rely entirely on electric power.

1895: George Westinghouse builds the world's first generating plant designed to transmit power over longer distances—a hydroelectric plant at Niagara Falls to

transmit alternating current some 20 miles to consumers in Buffalo, New York.

1901: The United States Steel Corporation is formed by a merger of several American companies.

Japan opens its first major iron and steel works.

1929: The U.S.S.R. begins implementing its first Five-Year Plan, which places nationwide industrial development under central government control.

Power generators at Edison Electric

1875: Japan builds its first railway.

1876: In the U.S. Alexander Graham Bell invents the telephone.

German inventor Nikolaus Otto produces a practical gasoline engine.

1870s: Sweden's railroad boom.

1883: Brooklyn Bridge completed.

1885: Germans Gottlieb Daimler and Wilhelm Maybach build the world's first motorcycle.

1886: Daimler and Maybach invent the carburetor, the device that efficiently mixes fuel and air in internal combustion engines

1888: The first electric urban streetcar system begins operation in Richmond, Virginia.

1893: American brothers Charles and J. Frank Duryea build a working gasoline-powered automobile.

1896: Henry Ford builds a demonstration car powered by an internal combustion engine.

1896–1904: Russia builds the Manchurian railway in China.

1903: Henry Ford establishes Ford Motor Company.

1904: New York City subway system opens.

Trans-Siberian Railroad completed.

1908: William Durant, maker of horse-drawn carriages, forms the General Motors Company.

1909: Ford introduces the Model T automobile.

1870: Parliament passes a law to provide free schooling for poor children.

1872: France bans the International Working Men's Association.

1874: France applies its child labor laws to all industrial establishments and provides for inspectors to enforce the laws.

1877: Wage cuts set off the Great Railroad Strike in West Virginia, and the strike spreads across the country. Federal troops kill 35 strikers.

1880: Parliament makes school attendance compulsory for children between the ages of 5 and 10.

1881: India passes a factory law limiting child employment.

1884: Germany passes a law requiring employers to provide insurance against workplace accidents.

1886: American Federation of Labor forms.

1887: U.S. Interstate Commerce Act passed to regulate railroad freight charges.

1890: The U.S. government outlaws monopolies with passage of the Sherman Antitrust Act.

1892: Workers strike at Carnegie Steel in Homestead, Pennsylvania, in response to wage cuts. An armed confrontation results in 12 deaths.

1894: The Pullman strike, called in response to wage cuts, halts American railroad traffic. A confrontation with 2,000 federal troops kills 12 strikers in Chicago.

1900: Japan passes a law to limit union activity.

1902: The United Mine Workers calls a nationwide strike against coal mines, demanding eight-hour workdays and higher wages.

1903: Socialists organize the Russian Social Democratic Workers Party.

1931: Japan passes a law to limit working hours for women and children in textile factories.

1870: The city-states of Italy unify to form one nation.

1871: Parisians declare self-government in the city but are defeated by government forces.

Prussia and the other German states unify to form the German Empire.

1877–1878: War between Russia and Turkey. Bulgaria gains independence from Turkey.

1900–1901: A popular uprising supported by the Chinese government seeks to eject all foreigners from China.

1917: Russian Revolution

1929: A worldwide economic depression begins.

67

GLOSSARY

ARISTOCRACY: rule by the upper class of society

BUREAUCRACY: the day-to-day running of government by officials who work for government agencies and departments

CAPITAL: money or property used in operating a business

CAPITALISM: the economic system in which property and businesses are privately owned and operated

CAPITALIST: a person who invests money in a business

CARTEL: an association of businesses that have joined together to organize a monopoly

CHARCOAL: a fuel made by charring wood in a buried fire so that very little air enters the fire

COKE: a form of coal that has been heated up to remove gases, so that it burns with great heat and little smoke

COMMON OR COMMONS: land in or around a village that any inhabitant may use

COMMUNIST: adhering to an economic system in which the community or government owns all property and operates all businesses

COTTAGE INDUSTRY: manufacturing goods at home

CZARIST: in Russian history the period of rule by monarchs called czars

DEPRESSION: decrease in business activity, accompanied by unemployment and lower prices and earnings

DYNASTY: a line of rulers who belong to the same family

ENCLOSURE: placing a physical barrier, such as a fence, around a piece of farmland to mark it as private property

FEUDAL: of the medieval system under which serfs worked on land held by a lord and gave part of their produce to the lord

GUILD: medieval form of trade association in which men in the same craft or trade organized to protect their business interests

INFRASTRUCTURE: underlying support, usually referring to the roads and other services provided to a community

LUDDITES: name given to English artisans who destroyed the new textile machinery that they feared would replace them; their imaginary leader was Ned Ludd

METALLURGY: the science of extracting metals from ores and refining them for use

MONOPOLY: exclusive right to control the purchase and sale of specific goods or services

PEASANT: rural dweller and farm worker

PER CAPITA: per person

PIG IRON: the product created by smelting iron ore in a furnace

PUDDLING: a process for converting pig iron to wrought iron by melting and stirring it

PUTTING-OUT SYSTEM: sending out work, such as spinning or weaving, to be done by workers at home

SELF-SUSTAINING: producing enough to support oneself

SERF: person living in servitude, legally bound to the land and its owner

SILK-THROWING: twisting together several long filaments of silk to make thread

SMELTING: melting metal ore to extract the pure metal

STATE-OF-THE-ART: most modern version

STEAM ENGINE: an engine that uses steam under pressure to produce power. In the most basic form of steam engine steam enters a cylinder and is then compressed with a piston.

TARIFF: tax on imports; duty

TECHNOLOGY TRANSFER: the movement of techniques and devices from one place to another

ADDITIONAL RESOURCES

BOOKS:

Crampton, Richard. *Atlas of Eastern Europe in the Twentieth Century*. New York: Routledge, 1997.

Hupchick, Dennis P. and Harold E. Cox. *The Palgrave Concise Historical Atlas of the Balkans*. New York: Palgrave MacMillan, 2001.

Moynahan, Brian. *The Russian Century: A Photographic History of Russia's Hundred Years*. New York: Random House, 1994.

WEBSITES:

http://www.alexanderpalace.org/mainpage.html
Alexander Palace Time Machine: images and essays about one of the czars who ruled Russia during its industrial revolution.

http://www.pbs.org/greatwar/
Companion site to a television program about World War I, including pictures and text.

http://vlib.iue.it/history/index.html
The Virtual Library-History Central Catalogue provides links to maps, biographies, and essays about each of the countries listed in the catalogue on the main page.

SET INDEX

Bold numbers refer to volumes

automobiles **8**:33–40

canals **3**:22–25, 34, 43; **5**:12–15, 18, 50; **9**:50–51; **10**:4–5

horse–drawn wagons **3**:16–20, 26–28; **5**:4–5, 8, 10, 28–30, 50; **7**:27, 30; **8**:5, 27

railroads **3**:15, 26–30, 42, 54–55, 61; **5**:17–18, 28–41, 50, 57; **6**:32–34, 53–56; **7**:18–20, 28, 30–31; **8**:4–7, 27–29, 52, 55; **10**:26, 40–41, 58–59

roads **3**:16–22; **5**:8–11, 29; **8**:36

steamboats **3**:30–33; **5**:17, 19–27, 50

urban **8**:50–51 **10**:52–54

Trevithick, Richard **3**:15, 26–28, 67; **5**:22

trusts **8**:30–31; **10**:56

turbines **3**:49; **5**:45; **6**:51; **7**:48–49

Turin, Italy **6**:26

Turkey **6**:37, 38, 40–41

U

unions **7**:21; **8**:15; **9**:10–12, 15, 51, 57, 60; **10**:5, 23, 28–31, 36, 38, 40, 42

American Federation of Labor **10**:30–31

American Railway Union **10**:40, 42

Knights of Labor **10**:28–30, 38

National Labor Union **10**:28

United Mine Workers **10**:38

United States

agriculture **4**:7–8, 58–59; **5**:39, 48; **8**:16–23, 59; **10**:18, 45, 56

child labor **4**:11, 13, 28; **8**:21; **10**:11, 14–16, 18–23

colonial period **4**:4–21

corporations **5**:57–61; **8**:31–32, 38–40, 42, 47–48, 51, 54; **10**:36, 39–42 56, 60–61

cottage industry **4**:7, 10–13; **10**:4, 18

environment **8**:9–12; **9**:37–38, 41;

10:48, 51–52, 60

factories **4**:24–27, 42–43, 46–48, 52; **5**:40, 44–47, 50; **7**:52, 61; **8**:55; **10**:6–8, 12, 17, 27, 34–35, 46–47

factory towns **4**:27–28, 34–35; **5**:42–54; **10**:39, 45

government and law **5**:16–17, 24; **8**:12, 31; **10**:20, 34, 36, 40, 56, 58–60

housing **5**:48–49; **10**:9–10, 56–59

immigrants **4**:5, 29, 59; **5**:48, 54; **6**:17–19; **8**:24, 64–66; **10**:10–11, 15–16, 23, 45

industrial accidents **5**:24, 35–37; **7**:58; **8**:14–15; **10**:12–13, 15–16, 19

iron and steel industry **4**:14–17, 23, 52–55, 61; **5**:39; **8**:52–53, 55, 58–59; **10**:24, 26, 60

mining **8**:10–15; **10**:18–19, 22–23

oil industry **8**:4, 26–31; **10**:56

population **4**:5, 16, 60; **5**:4–7; **8**:11; **10**:45

poverty **4**:4, 58; **8**:22–23; **10**:5, 8, 10, 56

strikes and protests **5**:48; **8**:54; **10**:5, 24–25, 29–31, 34–42

textile industry **4**:11–13, 19, 22–29, 40, 44–45, 49, 58–59; **5**:42–54, 53–54; **10**:6–8, 17, 27, 46–47

transportation **5**:4–5, 8–15, 17–41, 50, 57; **8**:4–7, 27–29, 33–40, 50–52, 55; **10**:4–5, 26, 40–41, 52–54, 58–59

unions **8**:15; **10**:5, 23, 28–31, 36, 38, 40, 42

women **4**:11, 28; **5**:48–49; **10**:11

Ure, Andrew **9**:20–21, 46

V

Van Buren, Martin **5**:24

Venice, Italy **6**:22–23

Verviers, Belgium **3**:40

Victoria (queen of Great Britain) **9**:8, 41